THE WALL WILL TELL YOU

THE
WALL
WILL TELL
YOU

The Forensics of Screenwriting

———

HAMPTON FANCHER

MELVILLE HOUSE
BROOKLYN · LONDON

The Wall Will Tell You
Copyright © Hampton Fancher 2019
All rights reserved

First Melville House Printing: March 2019

Melville House Publishing   Suite 2000
            46 John Street   and   16/18 Woodford Rd.
Brooklyn, NY 11201   London E7 0HA

mhpbooks.com
@melvillehouse

ISBN: 978-1-61219-761-6
ISBN: 978-1-61219-762-3 (eBook)

Designed by Marina Drukman

Printed in the United States of America

1 3 5 7 9 10 8 6 4 2

A catalog record for this book is available from
the Library of Congress

for Micheal Glass

Preface by Jonathan Lethem   ix

Start   1

Ink and Blood   7

Wheels   15

Heroes and Villians   21

The Bed and the Wall   31

Paint, Film, Bodies   39

Form   45

Fuck Up   51

Fuck It Up   59

You   63

HAMPTON'S WALL

Hampton Fancher is one of my favorite humans, an exception to the rule of what's possible in the art of living a life, an exception that makes you want to live a little bigger and a little harder. He's a teenage Flamenco runaway child star sidekick cowboy beatnik arm-candy countercultural Zelig patchouli-drenched shy handsome provocateur of a man, which isn't to mention: film director, documentary subject, screenwriter of *Blade Runners*, and author of a collection of remarkable short fiction, as well as author of moments in the lives of his friends they can only recall with dazed wonder. I'm not going to be able to tell you all I want to tell you about Hampton Fancher, about what it is to know him and care for him and be drawn into his universe, but that's okay, because we have this here book to consider instead. It is tempting to call *The Wall Will Tell You* a sequence of zen koans in the guise of a writer's guide, and it is that, but it is also something like a little brick hurled at the reader by the Ignatz Mouse part of Hampton. It is meant to lodge at an odd angle in your psyche and go on throbbing there, reminding you that the greatest cause in life is that of remaining delighted and remaining surprised, and putting that delight and surprise into whatever you do, and to offer it forth into the commons of the human. I've learned a lot from Hampton over the years, and most of all when what he had to teach me came in the form of a baffled admission that he had no fucking idea what to do from one moment to the next except live, write, exist, and love. I think it's all here for you now, if you want to take it.

—Jonathan Lethem

START

A screenplay is the bones
of a poem and the poem is a movie
and the movie is a dream.

Writing is improvising, is getting inside other minds, other voices. Practice listening, imitate other voices. Listen to people talk, watch people listen. Inhabit their feelings, take note of strangers and people you disdain. It will open the ear to your heart, your imagination, empower you with other voices. Writing is acting.

■

A character concerns us because of what she does, what she says and that she says it in situations the outcomes of which are uncertain. Most importantly it be a story that you, you the writer, really like.

■

Don't just point to the thing in the window; go into the store.

■

Take us somewhere. Dangle a promise. A question to be resolved. An impending event. Incidents, yes, but no incidentals.

■

A decisive event. Try beginning with one. One that leads to an unexpected challenge to the protagonist. Sudden change. Something that can go either way, will concern us, make us care about what might happen next. Hang us from the cliff, but for that to be a dramatic option there must be circumstances that support it. Your job is to invent a *destiny* for these characters.

■

Cause and consequence. Without the former you can't have the latter.

■

If there's nothing at stake you're dead. Uncertainties are good for narrative. The trouble their motives get them into, or unexpectedly shit happens out of nowhere. Watch some Preston Sturges. Open it up. Flail or bask in the divide between appealing and appalling. Squeeze it, widen it.

■

Disruption. Something that feels irreparable. The damage done. A circumstance your character is trapped in, is partly to blame for, then has to do what she has to do to overcome it. All of us have done it. Maybe not big things, but little ones are good. These are stories that can come to you lying on your back.

■

Have your characters live in chance. Living in the unknown means they have to take chances.

■

It's what might be under the rug that's compelling, but that's only if the rug is too. Oceanic, sweeping. Raft of the Medusa. Thomas Hart Benton meets Salvador Dalí. Think about it. Do it.

■

Locate the potential for tension. Where does it reside? The trouble you're in if you can't really find it is exactly where the process of trying to discover it begins. The characters have to be *persuasive*. But they won't be if the problems that challenge them are not. Persuasion has to take on life.

■

Construct truth through lying, make things up. Be free to lie, love to lie, exercise it. It ain't logic, it's instinct. Monkey around.

■

Identify/recognize the problems, the solutions. I mean in the narrative, see if you have any: it's a groping process, little certainty in it—chance and inspiration. It starts with dissatisfaction, with squinting—trying to reach things out of reach—on tiptoes, jump and grab, then write it clear and concise.

■

A weed in a windless place dying for a breeze. Write a dialogue between that weed and the sky and make that weed smart enough to connive a reluctant sky into whipping up a wind and the sky is no pushover.

■

What's usually needed in screenplaying is the directitude of a journalist. And the opposite of course, a dreamer too.

INK and BLOOD

"Wonder is the first of all
passions. It has no opposite."
— René Descartes

If you're not in love with words why are you writing? Wondrous, the books that explore the words, words that lead to ideas and ideas to expression. It is to your benefit to read a thousand books in your lifetime, and to get there you need to always be reading. Imagination is a greedy little pig that needs to be hand-fed. Several times a day. Fatten the pig.

■

If you're not in love with the construction of words, trying to be a writer is as futile as trying to find water in a desert. By memorizing great writing—the lines, the speeches, the dialogues of the poets and dramatists— you'll be keeping inside you the best company, the highest teaching. It will restore your heart, reward your mind, and provide immediate inspiration. Through recitation you can prime your faculties to write dramas wherever—on the subway, in the car, on the street, in the dentist's chair. "If there is any substitute for love, it's memory. To memorize, then, is to restore intimacy." Joseph Brodsky wrote that.

■

Ink and blood. Ink means the actual writing, putting the story to the page. There is good ink, which draws me into the narrative, and there is bad ink, which loses me. Blood is what brings to life drama and depth of the story; the viability and plurality of its characters. You can have intriguing characters that exist within an otherwise flat or confusing story—that's bad ink. You can have a good story with many dynamic elements, but acted out by characters who fail to pump the blood.

■

Explore ways to improve your writing of dialogue by asking *what should I have said* instead of *what did I say.* We walk away from situations all the time saying to ourselves, *Damn, I wish I had said this instead* of that. That's dialogue. Pay attention to it. Making notes on this stuff is one way you'll learn to write better dialogue. Pay attention to how you say what you say in your head, trust that it's the best way to put something to writing. And make a habit of writing these things down, otherwise you'll be stuck in your head and that might drive you nuts.

■

Plot is fate. Fate is inevitable. There can be no fate without characters whose fate concerns us. So for now forget plot except how it grows from character—the plight of your characters.

■

Every principal character has an enterprise. Question it. If it's not there the character won't move. There's got to be more than what just meets the ear.

■

There'll be no incentive to turn the page if there's no expectation of a destination. No matter how extraordinary the event described, it will only be ordinary if it's not consolidated within a plight of a character whose action concerns us. What is it that impedes, compromises, jeopardizes the concerns of the character? Locate the actionable conflict. The trick is to impede the character, not the reader. Make it difficult for the character, simple for the reader.

■

Too much talk and not enough trouble is a bad thing to do. Exposition should be disguised, hidden in the trouble. Don't be explaining things. Get rid of elaboration, keep the ball in the air, wake up the story. Draw a tree of your story. Climb the tree.

■

Mystery, discovery, a revealment. Is it achieved, even a little? A little goes a long way. But you're in trouble if there's no trouble they're in.

■

Linkage: a chain of events, without a chain the wheels won't turn.

■

The aqueduct. It's got purpose. Its structure is a function of its purpose. To convey something that moves, moves from A to whatever letter you want it to end on.

■

The anticipation of an *event*: the principals have been put on notice. And we await the outcome. Something expected, something that threatens to reveal or change the fate of one or more of the characters.

■

Drama is contraction/expansion, momentum based on the frustrated necessities of the characters. Their woes, agendas, liabilities and strengths, virtues, hopes and contradictions.

■

Progression, being on the way to something, somewhere, leaving somewhere, wanting, needing something. Don't dawdle, amble, or dillydally. Clarify, stay with the objective. There are exceptions, but if you digress, it better be pertinent to something your story or characters are up to. And digression better be fun. Above all, don't fucking digress into anything intellectual. It's action you want. It's a pinprick even. Keep it simple, keep it felt. Language is secondary. But it also isn't—don't be stupid, write sharp.

■

The conflict between harmony and invention will lead you to the inevitable in unforeseen ways.

WHEELS

A screenplay should hit the ground running.
In medias res—land in the middle of it—is a good idea.

Forward motion. Like a musical scale. Like an arrow. A leap. A run. A fall. Become the servant of your sensations. Write poetry! Where does *work* come from? Comes from the inside going out, the outside coming in. All is adaptation. Adapt the novel of your life, not your history, but your reactions, your ideas, into screenplay.

■

How do you get a person, a reader, a character, or you yourself to care about what happens next? For one thing, by something about to happen next.

■

Poignancy of character/place/activity/dialogue. Robust but delicate. Fussy and selective, alchemical. You have to alter things to accelerate them otherwise they stand still. Death is the performance, life is waiting for the show to start.

■

Impel. Impede. Impend. You want your characters to be impelled and then impeded and there will then be something impending.

■

The story will emerge from the *facts*, if the facts that constitute the story are believable. Not expositional facts, but circumstantial facts that lead smack into temptation and stress. The cat sat on the dog's mat. Falling in love with a man married to her best friend. The facts wrestling with need. The hot confusions of love and greed, of story.

■

In screenplaying aspire to travel lightly and keep moving. The ballast that keeps the narrative from capsizing and maintains the course is the character's intention. A sense of the inevitable should be taking shape two pages into anything. Something pending.

■

Exposition is the bugbear of screenplay writing. Best be sly with that, don't open your hand. The closed one is more enticing.

■

One key to narrative is the dynamic of struggle. Something has to have happened, or is about to happen.

■

The longer the answers to compelling questions are delayed, the more time and action there is for intrigue to boil over. But this presupposes that there's a predicament that intrigues.

■

Foreseeable, but not foreseen. What happens is unexpected, but what happens makes sense when it does. *Does* is the key. *Do* turns the lock. Characters in a movie have to move, they have to be doing something that leads to something.

■

Don't explain in dialogue what it is your story is trying to illustrate. If you resort to that you won't have a story. Let the story tell itself.

■

What has caused the event. The conditions. Do the results lead to new events, another result? They better. Reversal of fortune comes from the trouble the choices they make to get out of trouble lead them into. They are up against something and not just talking about it. Finding a way through and out of trouble is what fascinates our attention. Our job is to invite the reader into a space that makes them sit down and listen, to give them thing after thing worthy of their watching. If you're not doing that, you are not doing the job.

■

Reject the obvious transparent approach. Welcome the underhanded, that which is discovered through experimentation, engaging with your creativity. I'm not talking about formulas that break the mold, I'm talking about scrutinizing the mold itself.

HEROES and VILLAINS

Actor questions are the writer questions:
what are the imperfections and liabilities, the
virtues and charms of your characters?
The background. If they have none they are
not characters. They won't do or speak. They'll
move around like dolls in dead air.

Characters have principal characteristics. They respond to circumstances according to their natures so that what they do and say is intrinsic.

■

People (characters) let us know what they want us to know, want us to believe. The rest is a secret. Locate the secret. The hidden. The suffering. The ambitions. The blind spots. Pride can blind. Obsession can blind. Stupidity can blind. Desperation can blind. Overconfidence can blind. Timidity. Fear. Frustration. Perfectionism. Impatience. In other words, the traits, characteristics, idiosyncrasies of three-dimensional people. Your characters.

■

However concerned you are with your work, make your characters even more so, more concerned with what they're doing. And *doing* is everything. Important question: what is their concern? Your character might not be more than a name and a physical description, but give a concern to that name. Their cause can be trivial or profound, but harness them to it.

■

Your characters and stories can be elliptical, elusive, but never irrelevant. Measure all they do and say in light of that. Give the character you disagree with, disapprove of, a good case.

■

Appeal is essential. It comes from how your character handles a given situation. Find the dignity in every character. Invest them with conviction. Opposing convictions, silent or loud, opposite temperaments. Hassle, big or small, creates interest. No hassle, no interest.

■

Don't give characters flaws that you don't care about, that you don't take seriously, or that you don't think are fun.

■

Allow and encourage the enemy to have the intelligence to understand his/her opponent—and vice versa.

■

Hannibal's relationship to Agent Starling. Villainy is irresistible because her attraction and his repulsion are in tandem.

■

Characters have opinions. And you too, should have opinions about the characters. Tell yourself what those opinions are.

■

Endow your characters with imagination. Imagine their imagination. A person who approaches a subject with imagination is beautiful. Tom Wingfield in *The Glass Menagerie* is beautiful, he describes the condition of the people who lived through the Great Depression like this: "their fingers pressed forcibly down on the fiery Braille alphabet of a dissolving economy," etc. When he speaks his mind, he uses his imagination.

■

Is your character persuasive, is he persuading anybody of anything? Endow the fuckers with conviction. Activate them.

■

Everybody is right. Everybody is wrong. Sounds like truth, at least provisionally. Whatever it is, it puts characters in trouble. Righteousness with clay feet holding up convictions either to be laughed at, embraced, or alarmed by.

■

The emotional condition of a character can fuel a motive. In fiction, belief is where the fun begins. And the fun is the trouble the character is in. But you have to believe it. If you're on the wrong side of the belief divide, often, no matter what you do, it's going to be fatuous.

■

Introduce a new element, a surprise, a new character that ignites the old story into a better one. You can do anything you're inspired to do. Your villain can be honest and intelligent. The hero a liar and not very bright.

■

Come up with an extraordinary event between two people. Something that really happened or make it up, even if it is outlandish. Then do a little dialogue that results from that event. A forty-year-old man who develops romantic feelings for his eighty-year-old mother. What dialogue would come out of him confessing this to her?

■

The outward life and the inward life. The former is action. The latter is contemplation. Try to imagine someone else's vision. The water park of your character's mind.

■

Beware of unearned emotional reaction on the part of your characters. Simple dilemmas they can't get out of are good. Stuff that makes them fudge, makes them lie. But never hearts on the sleeve, they're a bore. The hidden heart is more revealing.

■

Your characters are not just puppets mouthing your first excuse at dialogue. They have their own agendas. Ulterior motives. It's not about what's on the desk, but what's hidden in the drawer.

■

In the psychology of the creation of the characters, one question worth the asking might be, Where is the self-interest? Such a question will dig a touch deeper into understanding that actionable term, *intention*. How they talk, how they act, and what they hide.

■

Two distinct points of view. Opposing needs. The contention of separate agendas. Look at deceit. Look at a happily married person who cannot tell his mate the truth. Look at neglect. At the conflict of possession versus freedom. Look at the misunderstood. Look for what's at the heart of a dilemma. Look for the hidden wound. At the disadvantaged trying to get the advantage.

■

What makes a story is what makes it worth telling. What is it that wakes shit up? What animates the inert? A promise of good things. And the opposite does too. Clarify those things, simplify them. And do it with a little elegance, please.

■

Consequences are earned by what precedes them. What's the incentive? What triggers your character to action? Try to stay with that, with what is present in your characters. Aspirations result in implications. The aspirations of your characters will create implications that result in consequences that in turn result in new implications.

■

Good intentions don't mean much unless they lead to trouble—funny or dangerous trouble. Bad intentions. Deception. Vengeance. Greed. Looking for payoff. But intentions nonetheless. Never less. Intentions lead to more. A mission. Anything can happen. A transfiguring event whose effects are uncertain keeping what's at stake from turning worse.

■

Be vigilant to see the difference between what is emotionally moving and what is just sentimental. Burn the banners, don't raise them. Fuck polemics.

THE BED and THE WALL

You write a scene the same way you make the bed,
when you make the bed with care.

Aspire to distillation. Extract the essentials, concentrate on those and throw the rest away.

■

Take whatever time it takes to write a good scene. Whatever time it takes, take it. It sets a standard for the next scene.

■

The elements need to complement and collide as they move toward a reckoning. Like a joke, it has to stay on course. What scenes do or don't do to serve the anxiety of expectation. A movie story is all about anticipating something, something about to happen.

■

Establish a new and surprising context before the proceeding scene. A disturbance of or a diversion from the narrative can lure it into less predictable territory.

■

Compression: we call them *movies* because they're supposed to move! Be abrupt and ride two rails, one suggestive, the other concise. It comes at you and it's gone.

■

Concentrate your efforts, your approach on what's going on immediately, which means *now*! Abruption! Something is happening!

■

Somebody wants to get there. Somebody else wants to stop him. Hence the drama of opposing strategies which make for moment-to-moment suspense. The goal is established, it's out there, but the route is uncertain. The clash of unintended consequences. Football. Dynamics of drama and comedy have to do with juxtaposing agendas.

■

A real bird doing a real thing.
An unreal bird doing a real thing.
A real bird doing an unreal thing.
An unreal bird doing an unreal thing.

■

Alarmed at a blast from the left, we look to see what it was and we're hit from a blast on the right.

■

If the character is not up against it enough to try to change it, you're on dry land. Especially if all they do is talk about what they're doing instead of doing it. Do it. Strike a match to the fireworks of misunderstanding. The unwanted. The mistreated. Jeopardize the goal of their desire. Their frailties and defenses can make them sharp, incarcerate them in the drama. Put blood on the page.

■

Take the short road. Use high octane. Sleek as a good joke. I'm talking about scenes.

■

Read your scene to an honest person. Encourage that person to help you locate the stumbling blocks. The weak points. Then turn stumbling block into cornerstone. Identifying stumbling blocks will lead you to the creations of cornerstones. Facile to say, hard to do, but that's our job.

■

If you question a scene, watch it on the screen. Your wall. Everybody's got one. Literally look up at your wall and watch the scene play. No picture, no story. Look at it critically. Does it run somewhere or just lie down and die? The wall will tell you.

■

Does it drag? If so, why? Maybe the thing is unmotivated, no struggle. Even a free floating balloon is on a dramatic journey. Will it rise or fall? Disappear or crash? Our concern with its fate is what it's about.

■

The meaning of real. Hold that up to what you do. Making the unreal real. You make it up. A story. Tell one to someone. Make it up. If it doesn't capture them, if they don't believe it, you didn't do it. But do it. Try it. I knew an actor who told some people that he was from another planet. Some people believed him. He wasn't a great actor, but if he hadn't died, he might have been. I just made up a story. Did you believe it?

■

Be blind to the commonplace. Avoid the stereotypical! Unclutter your prose. You may have a gift of being able to write dialogue with white, sharp teeth, but that's nothing if your descriptions lack bite. Go quicker, don't write everything your imagination sees—forget the fucking chairs and couch and what the flowers look like. Omit!

■

Look *into* the mystery of mundane details, the magic of place, the possibilities of everyday absurdity, snapshots instead of masterpieces might encourage the humanity, the dignity, insanity, or inanity of this cake you make. The sorriness underlying the grandest things. The grandeur underlying the sorriest things, Thomas Hardy said.

PAINT, FILM, BODIES

Music, painting, acting, architecture,
fucking pottery, even screenplay writing; in all art,
an element of surprise is essential.

Overcoming the problem of painting the picture while also explaining the picture in paint. The trick is, don't explain it. Dramatize what you write in your writing. Make it actionable, turn it into an event. Try to *see* what you are writing about. I don't mean paint an explicit word picture of bodies or even involve their bodies. I mean you must know it as well as you know the stranger or acquaintance next to you.

■

Can you think of a person without thinking of their body? There are historic figures that you apprehend through their intelligence, their convictions, their ideas, but either way you get it from either an impression or an image. You best have both to make a rendering of your characters.

■

Directing is about taking chances, being willing to improvise, being adaptable. Taking advantage of what the location, the weather, the moment might suddenly offer. To watch and listen, to shoot film like an ornithologist watches birds. And it's about understanding and perceiving the strengths and the weaknesses of the actors and quietly supporting them at either end. It's about being modest and strong at the same time. Don't give up till you like what you shot, but also try to have a good time doing that.

■

A good screenwriter should know a good director, and knowing a director means knowing what kinds of work he or she responds to, what he or she might want to shoot. Be prepared, though, to have your screenplay rewritten, even by another writer who can spot the problems you have been blind to.

■

That troubling path between too much information and not enough is a good place to work in. Like making your way through a darkened room, you hurry to find the light, a way out, but you better be careful, you could crash into something or fall off an unseen edge. But careful you can't be; you have to move.

Select and condense; most of all, tell a story, as much in "film" (for the eyes) as in dialogue. So what you write down you should try to see, not from within, but up on the wall. I already said that. I say it again. Imagine the screen and see how it looks. What you need and don't need: that's the test.

■

We think of each other's essence as reflected through the body of our physical presence. Articulate the mind and the flesh of the character; either intuitively you have a handle on your character or you have the objectivity to realize and to admit to yourself that you don't. Hence you go on the hunt, armed with questions to track the spoor of your unformed invention till it surprises you with its full-bodied presence, and is no longer just a puppet waiting for your voice and your hand to make it move, but instead jumps to life on its own volition and starts talking to you.

■

Thornton Wilder said that experiencing actors on stage is the most immediate way in which a human being can share with another the sense of what it is to be a human being.

■

Art doesn't explain, it demonstrates.

FORM

Dexterity. The compression of circumstance.
Context creates velocity, compression.
Look into the circumstance that your characters
inhabit. Cause and effect create form.

Forget the jelly, concentrate on the toast. Don't try for sublime. Bauhaus as opposed to baroque.

■

To build form out of a vision incubated in your invisible, internal world, then delivered into the visible external one, means that it must have a form. That sounded tautological because it is. So is sculpture, which also must have a coherent shape, a dynamic one that repeats certain curves, that moves up and down, in to out, that fluctuates, but holds together, whether its parts are obvious or elliptical. Your inspiration must have form in order to function.

■

And then there's also Rube Goldberg. A complex series of steps, of efforts, that arrive at a plain and simple result. A logical pattern (form) no matter how harebrained, that leads to a logical resolution, even if the conclusion is ambiguous or absurd.

■

The laws of proportion: nothing runs without form, wing-to-weight ratio has to be right or the plane won't fly. Then there's the opposite: wild, radical, improbable risk. The thrill of danger has an arm around humor.

■

The term *karma* means an unbroken sequence of cause and effect, each effect being, in its turn, the cause of a subsequent effect. The structure of a good screenplay must be filled with comprehensive karma.

■

Jeopardy. Plotline. *Psycho*: Janet Leigh steals money. In a simple *plot* is where you'll find the potential for turbulence. Otherwise it remains uncooked. Plot will allow you to cook it. Will give you *heat*. It should be very simple, very clear, concrete. Something at stake. Don't let people say too much. Do too much. Yet, they must strive. A simple shape. The facts will hopefully give you the simple shape to make a drama of it.

■

Get to the inner by depicting the outer. See it, hear it, describe it. A writer is a detective on the lookout for evidence, screenplaying is forensics.

■

Turning a novel into a screenplay is a reductionary exercise. A consolidation of characters. A crash diet. Novels are heavyweights. Screenplays, bantamweight, light-footed, and fast. A flower doesn't resemble the ground it grows in. An omelet comes from an egg, but doesn't look like one.

■

A screenplay is not generalization. It has to be singular, specific. Each little piece a solid rung, every page a step on the ladder you climb to the top at the end.

■

More of one thing instead of ten different things.

■

A lack of abruption is as predictive as pavement. It needs obstruction. Also, watch out for backstory, best it should unfold in real time.

FUCK UP

Half the battle is being able
to recognize that what you wrote and
thought was great is shit.

After you write a bunch of pages, distance yourself and if you can, see if what you've written still interests you—this writing you found on a bus seat somebody else wrote. John Gardner said it: to be "at once driven and indifferent."

■

You've made it out of matchsticks, made it all too plain and simpleminded and hence not succeeded in intriguing us. You've intrigued yourself maybe, but too easily. Turn out the lights, use a flashlight.

■

Your characters are uninteresting, flabby, unreal, predictable, stupid. You don't go far enough. You give up before you start by accepting the first thing that comes to mind. Do not settle for stereotype. Deepen it, expand it. The goodhearted bitch. The angel who hates himself. The introverted exhibitionist. Consider opposites, contradictions.

■

The reason screenplays are usually so bad is because of myopia. I've read screenplays by smart people, smart and renowned novelists, and very often they stink. It's myopia.

■

Myopia is the big liability. All the dumb stuff we do is because we're so close to it, we can't see that it's dumb, can't see it properly. Fine, do a little close-up work and then take a seat in the bleachers. Sure, you have to be a believer to do the work, but the work needs to be vetted agnostically.

■

To write good dialogue you must be capable of recognizing your failure to achieve it—that's a promising starting point—to know the difference between what is working and what isn't.

■

Style. Deadpan is better than ornamental, it better suits film writing. The opposite of deadpan is the refuge of the inept. Your ineptitude is the failure of your attempt to envision your story.

■

What it's about is nosedives. No doubt about it, you're going to crash, then what you have to do is put in more flight time. Become a nose diver and you'll learn to fly. Try to make a life of trying. You want to be smart and successful, but what you are is not so smart and you fail, and if you're so afraid of being a failure and you don't try not to be, a failure is what you'll be. When you're failing is when you're learning. Learning how you failed teaches you how to succeed.

■

If you get defeated by failure, you are not taking advantage of it. Failure leads to inspiration. Disappointment in your work, if you don't stop working, leads you to quality. Hence, make failure a function of your incentive. You can't get close to perfection except by standing on a stockpile of failure. The more open you are to failure, the closer you are to achievement. When you feel lonely and calamity is breathing down your back, in the darkness of yourself, this is the time, if you have the courage, to start groping, where you'll start to sense the shapes of some truth, of reality, poetry. This is where you will get the power to make something good.

■

Learn to become good at finding the extent of your failure in any given project or page. What works, what doesn't, and what may work by doing more work. Skirt your bullshit. Look for solid ground. It's a dialectical process, mental tennis. Heuristics.

■

Don't turn your back on failure. Pick it up, examine it carefully—your failure is your little orphan child and must not be neglected.

■

Never be precious. Never be nothing. Impose nothing. Force nothing. Samuel Beckett said it; "Forcing is fatal." And please, no big or even little unearned emotions. Check your stuff for anything stiff or repetitive. And remember, nothing worse than a message.

■

A collaborative exploration of that ambiguous territory separating bad work from good. Learn to locate and identify what obstructs you. A process that integrates the liberation of imagination with the necessity of structure is what this is about.

■

The rats of banality. Make sure not even one is hiding in your work.

FUCK IT UP

In the competition between apathy
and aspiration a wake-up question is,
How can I make it better?

What holds you back? Where does progress hide? How to change the patterns. The dream is dormant. How to wake it up is the thing. Desire. Explore. Stomp on the habits. Art is about loss. About the last time you cried.

■

The dreamer's logic is the dislogic of the dream. Get cozy with that.

■

In a room or the world or inside the head, it is fun, even compelling, to put the unfamiliar next to the common, something odd next to normal. Alchemy.

■

A screenplay should aspire to be a distillery—purified, concentrated, condensed. Just the essence of something moves it forward. Lingering is death. An elegant skeleton is better than a rotting corpse.

■

Screenplay prose should be lean, precise. Sharpen your phrases, make the dialogue sing. You don't want anything that doesn't have clear purpose. The character can shuffle from time to time, but not the writing. There shouldn't be an unsure word or pointless event in the whole screenplay. It's like a game of chess, the board stays the same, the rules are fixed—that's your skeleton—but the better player you are, the smarter choices you make within the game's endless possibilities.

■

A copycat will never be a lion.

YOU

You are in hock to your talent.
Redeem the pledge.

The Muse. The angel bitch. Don't be mean, don't be stupid, or she'll leave you. Keep your eyes open for presents she will like. Don't back down. Show her you're willing to play ball. You will be tested. Make her give you everything. It's a game of vigilance. Your affection for it means everything. Affection for what? For her, for your work. For the vision. She's elusive, tricky. So you too must be tricky. You throw yourself at her, body and soul, she kicks you in the head. Don't run, this just means that you must be sly, patient, seductive. She'll come around. She adores poetry.

■

The last line of a poem by Rilke about poor old Jacob wrestling with an angel and getting his ass kicked is instructive: *This is how he grows: by being defeated, decisively / by constantly greater beings.* Battle with the tough stuff.

■

To do anything that feels almost impossible and to do it consistently is always an act of will. Put your will into your works. Into the dream and the ideal of your days. This should be who you are, which is also being who you need to become.

■

Look for answers to your own questions, as if they were someone else's questions. It's the questions, stupid. You have to be a second person to yourself. Your own devil's advocate.

■

About the juggling of two elements. The ball of impulsivity and experimentation, of spontaneity and risk. But also the ball that plans what's next and has a result in mind, the goal. Keep your eyes on both. Two things, two eyes.

■

To get where you need to be, you need your heart to be in it. And see to it that your character has a heart as well. Something of a fanatic might be good.

■

The cause you serve is your story. A question to ask is whether or not you're better than the cause you serve. If you decide you are, then you're serving the wrong story. Remember, it's your actual soul that is struggling to dream this stuff up. Each thing you try is an assignment from down deep. Even if it doesn't feel like it—it is.

■

What you are trying to learn cannot be taught. What you learn is by teaching yourselves through trying. You have to become better than your teachers or your teachers are shit.

■

Here is a personal example with some critical drizzle. The logic of *The Minus Man* was about an indifferent victory. One without moral meaning, because finally life offers none. Trying to dramatize my conviction that it is impossible to get to the bottom of anything that has ultimate meaning—not that it's all meaningless, but that our natures remain elusive, mysterious. Not that I set out to prove that, but that was the process, the adventure of grappling with the invention. Of word and picture that felt like a far-off alarm. Dreamy desolation. Haunted solipsistic vacancy. The rustle of a nun's skirt. Panning the sterility of an empty sea town with serial music. A lullaby is a song you are not meant to hear the end of. Not going anywhere, but it doesn't stay put. A lack of purpose, a lark. A rattlesnake in an Easter basket. Cinema working for a dream. A silent relationship to the landscape delivered. Simple, smooth, but with touches of impact in the flatness of it all. Something will happen. Prelude to epilepsy. Odyssey of dislocation. Nobody has a mommy, not even Mommy. Nobody saved. Mars on Long Island. Climbing cables to nowhere.

ABOUT THE AUTHOR

HAMPTON FANCHER was born in East Los Angeles in 1938 to a Mexican-Danish mother and an American father. At the age of fifteen, he ran away from home to Spain to pursue a career as a Flamenco dancer. After returning to Los Angeles, Fancher began acting in the late 1950s, appearing in films such as *The Naughty Cheerleader*, in which he starred with Broderick Crawford and Klaus Kinski, as well as in innumerable classic TV shows of the era such as *Bonanza*, *Perry Mason*, *The Fugitive*, and *Mannix*. In the 1970s, Fancher began focusing on directing and screenwriting. He would go on to write the screenplay for *Blade Runner* (1982) and, thirty-five years later, its sequel, *Blade Runner 2049* (2017), as well as the Denzel Washington film *The Mighty Quinn* (1989) and the Owen Wilson movie *The Minus Man* (1999), which Fancher also directed. In addition to teaching screenwriting at New York University and Columbia University, Fancher has published a collection of stories, *The Shape of the Final Dog*. Described by the *Los Angeles Times* as "a world-class raconteur," Fancher was the subject of the recent, highly praised documentary *Escapes*.